LENTEN LESSONS

PREPARING FOR WORSHIP IN LENT

YEAR A

LENTEN LESSONS
Preparing for Worship in Lent
Year A

R. Kevin Johnson

MICAH PUBLISHING

Micah Publishing
P.O. Box 2332
Boone, North Carolina 28607

Micah Publishing is a division of Micah Ministries.

Unless otherwise noted, scripture quotations are from the *New Revised Standard Version Bible,* copyright © 1989 National Council of the Churches of Christ in the United States of America. Used by permission. All rights reserved.

Library of Congress Cataloging-in-Publication Data

Johnson, R. Kevin
   Lenten lessons : preparing for worship in Lent year A /
   R. Kevin Johnson.—1st ed.
   p. cm.
   ISBN 978-0-980062106 (pbk.)
                                              2007941085

Cover design and photography by R. Kevin Johnson

Printed in the United States of America

This collection of Lenten essays

is written in memory of

Robert E. Webber

who helped me understand

what it means to keep a holy Lent.

Contents

Acknowledgements

I am grateful to the congregation of First Baptist Church, Boone, North Carolina, who encouraged me during the completion of this project.

Special thanks go to Ida Miles for her work as copy editor, Janet Culley for administrative support, and to Wayne Brown, Joy Brown, and Dale Collie for their ongoing encouragement, words of wisdom, and prayers. Thanks are also due to Connie Cherry, Edna Grenz, and David Music for their kind endorsements.

As always, I am grateful to God for Marian, my partner in life and ministry. Without her love, prayers, encouragement, insights, suggestions, and Christian witness, this project would not have been possible.

Gratia et veritas,

R. Kevin Johnson

Preface

This Lenten devotional guide is designed in a way that allows worshipers to study the lectionary scriptures for corporate worship in advance of each Sunday. In Lent, four common scripture passages (Old Testament, Psalm, New Testament, and Gospel) are recited and preached in churches around the world. This workbook encourages the opportunity to reflect on each passage and also provides a guide to prayer during this holy season.

It is my prayer that the worship experiences of those who use this resource will be enhanced by the "homework" that is done before meeting with other believers to worship corporately.

Ash Wednesdays

Year A

Feb 6, 2008
March 9, 2011
March 5, 2014
March 1, 2017
Feb 26, 2020
Feb 22, 2023
Feb 18, 2026
Feb 14, 2029
Feb 11, 2032
Feb 7, 2035
Mar 10, 2038

Ash Wednesday

Read: Matthew 6:14-18

On Ash Wednesday, Christians around the world seek out churches in order to have the ash from burned palm fronds (generally those used in the church on the previous Palm Sunday) pressed onto their foreheads in the shape of a cross. As ministers preside over this imposition of ashes, they tell penitents "remember you are dust and to dust you shall return."

For many people, this act begins the process of forty-six days of reflection, remembrance, and introspective spiritual renewal. In order to focus attention on this time, many give up an ordinary activity of life and substitute the time they would spend on that activity in a time of prayer and fasting.

In addition to seeking to prepare and repair one's own heart and mind, Lent is the perfect time to search the heart to examine human relationships with both Christians and non-Christians. The scriptures are filled with the hope of the promise of the Savior—saying that when we are faithful and gracious enough to forgive others who wrong us in some way, the Lord is faithful to forgive each of us of our sins.

However, in the process of seeking holiness

during a season of sacrifice, many moan and groan, such that others will, as the scripture says, "see that they are fasting." During this beautiful season, however, we are called to joy— recognizing our faults, but acknowledging the forgiveness that comes because a God who loves us was willing to send a Savior who died for us, that we might live in the shadow of his resurrection and know the fullness of his love, joy, peace, patience, kindness, goodness, faithfulness, gentleness, and self-control.

With that, we are invited to a holy Lent—one that draws us closer to the Christ as we remember his sacrifice for us on the cross.

Thursday after Ash Wednesday

Read: Genesis 2:15-17; 3:1-7

The first sin recorded in the scriptures is one of disobedience. God provided a lavish and lush dwelling place for Adam and Eve with one requirement: they must not eat the forbidden fruit. Of course, when tempted, the happy couple finds themselves busily disobeying the one who created them and gave them everything they were enjoying as the fruit of creation.

The direct metaphor to modern life is obvious. The first sin a child commits is disobedience. "No, no," and "don't do that," seem to be parental invitations to test both the authority and the tolerance of those who only have the toddler's best interests at heart. Ultimately, the parent corrects, the child succumbs to the discipline, and the child is set on the right path. Because of the punishment the child endures, she learns from her mistake and is far less likely to repeat the offense.

While sins can be confessed, repented of, and forgiven, there are nevertheless consequences for one's actions. The modern child loses privileges, and in our biblical story, so do Adam and Eve. They find themselves under the watchful eye of the Lord God; however, they lose the privilege of a life in perfect communion with him.

It is the peace of reconciliation that provides ultimate comfort to those who recognize their sinfulness and seek repentance. Suffering the consequences of sin is part of the process. That is the lesson of the Garden.

Friday after Ash Wednesday

Read: Psalm 32

During this season of Lent, the focus of Christians often turns to a remorseful time of penitence. All are called to a Holy Lent, a time of examination as one considers his condition before God.

Psalm 32 gives a picture of the benevolent God and shows both his greatness and goodness. In the Psalm, David describes a merciful God who gladdens the hearts of those who acknowledge their sins before him. There is assurance that "steadfast love surrounds those who trust in the Lord" (v. 10).

May God grant his people grace to seek the gladness of heart available to us because of the penitent hearts during this holy season.

Saturday after Ash Wednesday

Read: Romans 5:12-19

"But the free gift is not like the trespass. For if the many died through the one man's trespass, much more surely have the grace of God and the free gift in the grace of the one man, Jesus Christ, abounded for the many" (v. 15).

The life that Christians live is constantly under the influence of others. What is watched on television or at the movies, what is listened to on the radio, and who are chosen as close friends are all factors in who we are and who we ultimately become. It is often by our own influence that Christians can either cause another to grow toward maturity in Christ or become a stumbling block for another who may be struggling in the faith.

Our passage for today speaks to this troubling reality. It is by one that sin entered the world. Under the law, there was no hope of reconciliation. The influence of one caused the fall of many. Even so, the grace of God in the person and work of Jesus Christ allowed for all who were affected by the fall of just one man to be redeemed by just one man.

The First Sunday in Lent

Read: Matthew 4:1-11

In the gospel passage for the first Sunday in Lent, Jesus is led to the wilderness to be tempted by Satan. Jesus' first forty days in the wilderness were spent fasting and it was at the conclusion of this period, when Jesus was at his weakest physically, that Satan approached him to question his divinity. Satan attempts to appeal to Jesus on a very practical level; surely taking advantage of the humanness of the word became flesh.

Satan knows that Jesus is hungry so he gives him an idea about how to be fed. Satan then commands Jesus to throw himself from the top of the temple. Satan, knowing that Jesus is probably frustrated with the process and perhaps isn't thinking clearly, pulls out all the stops, counting on the greediness of human flesh to be the snare that entraps the Savior. He says, "If you worship me, you will have complete lordship and control over all the kingdoms of the world."

Jesus responds to each satanic challenge by quoting scripture—and, given that Jesus is in fact the Son of God and knows his Father intimately, he is able to draw strength over temptation when Satan puts him to the test.

Are we seeking to have the knowledge of the word of God and the strong personal relationship with him that will help us to overcome not only temptation, but also the various trials of life? At the height of battle when the stress and strain of spiritual warfare is most apparent, may we all, like Jesus recognize the angels who are steadfast to give us comforts and accept that holy grace.

Monday after the First Sunday in Lent

Today we reflect on the scriptures from the first Sunday in Lent. These passages point us both to the problem of and the solution to sin.

While we are able to understand the consequences of the fall of man, we are also given the assurance that God is our comforter, he offers us the free gift of salvation through his son, Jesus, and we begin to catch a glimpse of Jesus as we consider his role as an acceptable sacrifice to atone for the sins of humankind.

There is nothing that we go through in our daily lives that can compare to the temptations, the trials, and the heartache that Jesus experienced. It is the Jesus who is not only fully God, but also fully man who knows our weaknesses and keeps us in his care.

"For our sake he made him to be sin who knew no sin, so that in him we might become the righteousness of God" (2 Corinthians 5:21).

Tuesday after the First Sunday in Lent

Read: Genesis 12:1-4

What a perfect blessing is exhibited in this passage from Genesis. In it, God gives Abraham a command and a promise, and Abraham responds with an act of obedience. Abraham was called out to do something extraordinary: to leave the familiarity and comfort of home, for which he was blessed beyond measure.

At some time or another in life, all of us have to leave what we have always known as home. Teenagers go off to college. Young adults begin a first job in a new or unfamiliar city. People with extra time on their hands take on volunteer positions even though they are nervous and feel unqualified. In the case of many Christians, leaving home means answering the call of God even in the midst of timidity and with a feeling of unworthiness.

When God's people respond in obedience to the call on our lives, God blesses us beyond measure and is able to make a "great nation" through our respective witnesses of faith, service, and love. When Christians allow themselves to be used, the possibilities are endless.

During this season of lengthening days, may we all be willing to pour daylight onto our witness by our acts of absolute obedience to the Father, the God of Abraham.

Wednesday after the First Sunday in Lent

Read: Psalm 121

Some of my favorite things to sing in high school choir were excerpted from Mendelssohn's *Elijah.* The choral sequence to which Mendelssohn sets Psalm 121 is a beautiful trio of treble voices singing *a cappella:*

"Lift thine eyes, oh, lift thine eyes to the mountain whence cometh help. Thy help cometh from the Lord, the maker of heaven and earth. He hath said, thy foot shall not be moved. Thy keeper will never slumber."

The trio segues into a full choral setting of the text, "He watching over Israel slumbers not nor sleeps," with a flowing and soothing orchestral accompaniment.

I count Psalm 121 as one of the Bible verses to which I wouldn't have paid much attention (and certainly wouldn't have memorized) but for the ministry of a composer who felt led to tell the story of a great prophet.

In addition to this wonderful gift of song, the message of the passage gives me wonderful hope during Lent.

Help comes from the Lord—he is tireless. He requires nothing of me but to look to him and to trust him completely when I am in need of spiritual comfort.

God is my protector and my shield. God protects me from evil and he is with me wherever I go, guarding the paths on which I walk.

The wonderful thing about Psalm 121 is the final sentence of the passage. The eternal message of hope revealed in a simple answer to the question, "How long will this benevolence last?"

The answer? "From this time forth and forever."

Thanks be to God!

Thursday after the First Sunday in Lent

Read: Romans 4:1-5; 13-17

The season of Lent provides Christians with the wonderful opportunity to examine the relationship between who we say we are and how we behave as believers. It is one thing to say that we believe in the Christ; however, it is quite another thing to live in such a way that others realize that there is something different about our lives—something that they too desire.

While the things that we do and the way that we behave has nothing to do with attaining salvation through Christ, those things certainly advance the Kingdom of God by exhibiting Christian character, serving as an example of how one should live, and making the world a better place in which to live by doing acts of service and helping those in need.

The promise of salvation comes through belief and trust in the Lord. The joy of salvation is displayed by our expressions of that faith along the path of righteousness.

Friday after the First Sunday in Lent

Read: John 3:1-17

Long before I was able to read, I memorized scripture that I learned through music, at home and in Sunday school and Mission Friends. The first passage I memorized was from today's reading, John 3:16-17.

At the age of four, I would take my small Gideon New Testament around our church, open it to a random passage, and then recite this passage from the gospels as if I were reading to those gathered in earshot.

It was the simple truth of the gospel passage that could not be contained in the memory of a four year old. Instead, it flowed forth like a living stream and all who were close enough got splashed by the words of truth:

"For God so loved the world that he gave his only son, so that everyone who believes in him may not perish but may have eternal life. Indeed, God did not send the Son into the world to condemn the world, but in order that the world might be saved through him."

May God give us grace this Lent to share the truth of the gospel boldly and unashamedly.

Saturday after the First Sunday in Lent

Reflect on the scriptures studied this week with these questions in mind:

What theme(s) have I noticed in the scripture passages this week?

What do I anticipate learning in worship as the church gathers in community on Sunday?

How do I anticipate responding to God and his word in worship on Sunday?

What passage has God used to speak to me this week?

How is God calling me to a holier place in life during this Lenten season?

Lord, thank you for speaking through the scriptures in every generation. As our church gathers to worship on Sunday, draw us closer to yourself by uniting us around a common conviction by the power of the Holy Spirit. Amen.

The Second Sunday in Lent

Read: Matthew 17:1-9

Nothing is quite as good as obtaining affirmation from one that is loved and respected. More than that, when one is affirmed by another who is respected, that person becomes increasingly respectable.

In this Gospel passage, Peter, James, and John experience something extraordinary. Jesus is transfigured before their eyes and then he receives a ringing endorsement from the best references he could possibly have: Moses, Elijah, and his Father God.

The most striking affirmation of the ministry of Jesus comes in a three-part statement from the heavens. From the voice of God, Peter, James, and John learn that Jesus is, indeed, the Son of God! Secondly, they learn that Jesus is in the center of the will of the Father. Finally, the three are told to listen to the message that Jesus brings, fulfilling the words of the prophets.

The words from Father God created a sense of awe, fear, and reverence that drew the disciples to their knees. May the truth and relevance of this episode from the biblical narrative cause each of us to respond in the same manner.

Monday after the Second Sunday in Lent

Reflect on the past week of personal worship and worship in community with these questions in mind:

What can I give up in order to spend time in closer communication with God?

How has the Lord spoken to me through the scriptures this week?

How is God challenging me to a fuller life in Christ during this Lenten season?

What insights did I gain through worship in community this week?

Thank you, O God, for a week of personal and corporate worship. Draw me closer to you as I reflect on those things you have revealed to me through the scriptures by the power of the Holy Spirit. Amen.

Tuesday after the Second Sunday in Lent

Read: Exodus 17:1-7

God of Patience and Providence:

The Israelites quarreled with Moses and tested you in the midst of their frustration and thirst. The people hardened their hearts toward you. They rose up against your servant and threatened his life. Nevertheless, you provided for their every need and showed them time and again that you are Holy God.

During this holy season, teach us to be people of peace and reconciliation. Teach us to trust that you are always faithful to do exactly what you say you will do. Give us hearts with room for you to dwell. Grant us grace to be the people you have called us to be.

Deliver us, O God. Amen.

Wednesday after the Second Sunday in Lent

Meditate on Psalm 95:

O come, let us sing to the LORD; let us make a joyful noise to the rock of our salvation!

Let us come into his presence with thanksgiving; let us make a joyful noise to him with songs of praise!

For the LORD is a great God, and a great King above all gods.

In his hand are the depths of the earth; the heights of the mountains are his also.

The sea is his, for he made it, and the dry land, which his hands have formed.

O come, let us worship and bow down, let us kneel before the LORD, our Maker!

For he is our God, and we are the people of his pasture, and the sheep of his hand. O that today you would listen to his voice!

Do not harden your hearts, as at Meribah, as on the day at Massah in the wilderness, when your ancestors tested me, and put me to the proof, though they had seen my work.

For forty years I loathed that generation and said, "They are a people whose hearts go astray, and they do not regard my ways."

Therefore in my anger I swore, "They shall not enter my rest."

Thursday after the Second Sunday in Lent

Read: Romans 5:1-11

Recently, I found out that someone I know has been saying unflattering things about me to a mutual acquaintance. Among other things, this person told my friend that she and I have never gotten along. When word about this got back to me I was completely surprised. I had no idea that I didn't get along with this person.

As I thought about it, I recalled a misunderstanding that this person and I had a while ago. She let me know that I had offended her, I sat and talked with her about it, I apologized that her feelings had been hurt and I let her know that I had not intended to upset her or show her disrespect. She accepted my apology and said, "I forgive you and we shall never speak of it again." Several months later, I've learned that, while she and I haven't spoken of the instance again, she is nevertheless speaking about it to others and hasn't forgiven me as she said.

I am grateful that we Christians can take comfort in the fact that the Lord doesn't treat us that way. When we confess, ask forgiveness, and repent of our sins against God, the scriptures say that, "he is faithful and just to forgive us our sins and to cleanse us from all unrighteousness" (1 John 1:9). In the Psalms, we are also assured that, "As far as the east is from the west, so far has God removed our transgressions from us" (Psalm 103:12).

The incident I described above makes me mindful of the importance of Christ-likeness when dealing with those who have wronged us. It is imperative that we all follow the example of the Savior who is willing to show us grace beyond measure when we fall short. It is a beautiful thing to be able to say to a brother or a sister "I forgive you" and to mean it. It is even more beautiful to realize that doing so is to follow the example that Christ set for us.

"Much more surely then, now that we have been justified by his blood, will we be saved through him from the wrath of God. For if while we were enemies, we were reconciled to God through the death of his Son, much more surely, having been reconciled, will we be saved by his life. But more than that, we even boast in God through our Lord Jesus Christ, through whom we have now received reconciliation."

Friday after the Second Sunday in Lent

Read: John 4:5-42

This familiar story from the gospel can be retold from memory by any armchair theologian or small child fresh from Sunday school. Basically, it goes like this: Jesus is traveling on a hot day; he rests by a well while his disciples fetch lunch; a Samaritan woman comes to draw water; Jesus baffles her by his knowledge of her circumstances—past and present.

The woman was completely appalled that a Jewish man might speak to a woman of Samaria—particularly one with questionable values who is a bit of an outcast. She, therefore, questions Jesus' motivation and he shares information about another kind of water that will do much more than slake the average desert thirst. He tells her about the Living Water.

The dialogue continues with a discussion for the ages concerning worship style, and then the disciples return wide-eyed in disbelief over Jesus' willingness to minister even to those perceived to be the very least.

The conversation ends, the disciples go about picnicking, and the woman runs away without her water jar. The tool of her existence that meant so much to her just moments before was left sitting by the well because she had more important things to attend to. She had encountered the Savior. She was a changed woman. She had to tell others, "Come and see a man who told me everything I ever did and loved me still!"

The townspeople came running and many believed because of the witness of the one whom no one respected. The scriptures are clear to explain that the people didn't trust Jesus because of the woman; rather they were led to Jesus by the woman, and then Jesus did the rest.

This magnetic man called "Jesus" did the rest.

Saturday after the Second Sunday in Lent

Reflect on the scriptures studied this week with these questions in mind:

What theme(s) have I noticed in the scripture passages this week?

What do I anticipate learning in worship as the church gathers in community on Sunday?

How do I anticipate responding to God and his word in worship on Sunday?

What passage has God used to speak to me this week?

How is God calling me to a holier place in life during this Lenten season?

Lord, thank you for speaking through the scriptures in every generation. As our church gathers to worship on Sunday, draw us closer to yourself by uniting us around a common conviction by the power of the Holy Spirit. Amen.

The Third Sunday in Lent

Lord God:

Thank you for providing water to satisfy thirst when the Israelites hardened their hearts against you and doubted their presence among you.

Thank you for providing the Living Water that no one may thirst again if they put their faith and trust in you through your son, the Christ.

Deliver us, O God. Amen.

Monday after the Third Sunday in Lent

Reflect on the past week of personal worship and worship in community with these questions in mind:

What can I give up in order to spend time in closer communication with God?

How has the Lord spoken to me through the scriptures this week?

How is God challenging me to a fuller life in Christ during this Lenten season?

What insights did I gain through worship in community this week?

Thank you, O God, for a week of personal and corporate worship. Draw me closer to you as I reflect on those things you have revealed to me through the scriptures by the power of the Holy Spirit. Amen.

Tuesday after the Third Sunday in Lent

Read: 1 Samuel 16:1-13

One of the wonderful things about God is that he sees things differently than humans do. Because he is able to look beyond the outward appearance of man, God judges the people of his creation based on the condition of their hearts.

Such was the situation in the case of Samuel who was searching for the Lord's anointed. The seven obvious choices for king among the sons of Jesse were passed over. It was the young, handsome, beautiful-eyed David whom the Lord had anointed to be his king. When he passed before Samuel, he looked like a simple, young, hard-working boy; however, the Lord looked beyond David's outward appearance and knew that this boy was in fact a man after God's own heart.

"The Lord said, 'Rise and anoint him; for this is the one.' Then Samuel took the horn of oil, and anointed him in the presence of his brothers; and the spirit of the LORD came mightily upon David from that day forward" (v.12-13).

May God give us grace to be a people after God's own heart, operating solely for his purposes and seeking to be more than outward appearances indicate we might be for his Kingdom.

Wednesday after the Third Sunday in Lent

Meditate on Psalm 23:

The Lord is my shepherd, I shall not want.

He makes me lie down in green pastures; he leads me beside still waters;

he restores my soul. He leads me in right paths for his name's sake.

Even though I walk through the darkest valley, I fear no evil; for you are with me; your rod and your staff— they comfort me.

You prepare a table before me in the presence of my enemies; you anoint my head with oil; my cup overflows.

Surely goodness and mercy shall follow me all the days of my life, and I shall dwell in the house of the LORD my whole life long.

When I participate in worship services honoring a Christian who has died, the family of the departed often requests that this Psalm be recited by those who are gathered. The reason is obvious: the Psalm offers hope, peace, comfort, and assurance of life eternal.

43

However, my favorite sentiment when I reflect on the character of God displayed in this Psalm is that he is a shepherd. He is the one who steers or directs us back on to his intended route when we stray and he keeps us from wandering away when we doubt. He offers the tranquility that comes only in him and through his son Jesus, by the power of the Holy Spirit.

The Lord is my shepherd, I shall not want.

Thursday after the Third Sunday in Lent

Read: Ephesians 5:8-14

Both bulbs were out in the light fixture hanging in the hallway of my home. A week passed before I mustered the will to search for replacements on a forgotten shelf in the garage, remove the globe from the ceiling, properly dispose of the old bulbs, and wind the new energy-efficient bulbs into their cradles overhead.

It wasn't until I scrambled down from my perch and turned the light switch to the *on* position that I realized how much I had missed the light in the hallway. Suddenly, I was able to see everything clearly and I was able to move about freely and quickly without fear of bumping into a piece of furniture or turning my ankle on a misplaced dog toy.

When we walk as children of and in the light of Christ, we walk a road where everything is laid bare and is perfectly visible. It is by God's grace that sin exposed by this light is forgiven, and our faith is given legs to do the things that God would have us do for his purposes without fear of tripping in the darkness.

May God grant us grace to be a people of light as we receive the admonition, "Sleeper, awake!

Rise from the dead, and Christ will shine on you."

Friday after the Third Sunday in Lent

Read: John 9:1-41

When I was in grade school, my grandmother drove me to her house one afternoon. At that hour, the sun was easing down in the western sky and, as we topped a hill, my grandmother suddenly found herself blinded by the brilliant sunlight. She decided it was best to brake and pull off the road for a while until the sun set completely; however, the sun was so bright and the reflection through her bifocals so strong that she couldn't even see to maneuver the old Impala off the road.

This inability to see and my grandmother's decision to brake caused quite a traffic jam. Patient drivers moving in both directions on the two-lane road waited until I could use my limited vocabulary to direct my grandmother into the parking lot of a Mom and Pop's convenience store where we shared a Pepsi-Cola.

It is ironic that it is sometimes most difficult to see when we are dwelling in the brightest light. The expression "blinded by the light" certainly fit my grandmother's situation on the day I describe above, and it also fit the situation with the Pharisees the day that they interrogated the formerly-blind man.

The focus of their investigation centered on the fact that the person who did the healing, whoever he was, was a sinner because he did his work on the Sabbath. By seeking to shed light on the situation by dwelling on this point, the Pharisees found themselves even more deeply entrenched in darkness without ever realizing it.

"I came into this world for judgment so that those who do not see may see, and those who do see may become blind." Some of the Pharisees near him heard this and said to him, "Surely we are not blind, are we?" Jesus said to them, "If you were blind, you would not have sin. But now that you say, 'We see,' your sin remains."

Saturday after the Third Sunday in Lent

Reflect on the scriptures studied this week with these questions in mind:

What theme(s) have I noticed in the scripture passages this week?

What do I anticipate learning in worship as the church gathers in community on Sunday?

How do I anticipate responding to God and his word in worship on Sunday?

What passage has God used to speak to me this week?

How is God calling me to a holier place in life during this Lenten season?

Lord, thank you for speaking through the scriptures in every generation. As our church gathers to worship on Sunday, draw us closer to yourself by uniting us around a common conviction by the power of the Holy Spirit. Amen.

The Fourth Sunday in Lent

Illuminating Presence:

Give us grace to be children of light without being blinded by the light.

Help us to see others as you see them and to examine ourselves through your eyes.

Deliver us, O God. Amen.

Monday after the Fourth Sunday in Lent

Reflect on the past week of personal worship and worship in community with these questions in mind:

What can I give up in order to spend time in closer communication with God?

How has the Lord spoken to me through the scriptures this week?

How is God challenging me to a fuller life in Christ during this Lenten season?

What insights did I gain through worship in community this week?

Thank you, O God, for a week of personal and corporate worship. Draw me closer to you as I reflect on those things you have revealed to me through the scriptures by the power of the Holy Spirit. Amen.

Tuesday after the Fourth Sunday in Lent

Read: Ezekiel 37:1-14

Eternal God:

You rise up nations of people to serve you. You hang flesh on dry bones and breathe breath into senseless beings. You bring meaning to the meaningless. You bring hope to the hopeless. Your spirit dwells within your people and that alone brings life.

Deliver us, O God. Amen.

Wednesday after the Fourth Sunday in Lent

Meditate on Psalm 130:

Out of the depths I cry to you, O Lord.

Lord, hear my voice! Let your ears be attentive to the voice of my supplications!

If you, O Lord, should mark iniquities, Lord, who could stand?

But there is forgiveness with you, so that you may be revered.

I wait for the Lord, my soul waits, and in his word I hope;

My soul waits for the Lord more than those who watch for the morning, more than those who watch for the morning.

O Israel, hope in the Lord! For with the Lord there is steadfast love, and with him is great power to redeem.

It is he who will redeem Israel from all its iniquities.

Thursday after the Fourth Sunday in Lent

Read: Romans 8:6-11

This passage from Romans teaches that the Christian hope of eternal salvation comes not through mortal flesh. Instead, it comes by the Spirit, fed by righteousness, offering his indwelling presence as we cope with every circumstance of life.

The Christian hope is based on God's ultimate promise in Christ—a promise fulfilled in the birth of a Savior who lived to die. It is the Christ who became sin for us and shouldered our load. God's promise is sealed by Christ's Resurrection and Ascension. God did what he said he would do. Now Christians wait with hope and in expectation of the second-coming of our Savior.

For this, we can boldly proclaim:

"There is therefore now no condemnation for those who are in Christ Jesus. For the law of the Spirit of life in Christ Jesus has set you free from the law of sin and of death" (Romans 8:1-2).

Friday after the Fourth Sunday in Lent

Read: John 11:1-45

The Christian hope depends largely upon Christ's lordship in our lives. When we make Christ the Lord of our lives—that is, the Lord of all things concerning us—we allow him to control the future and we trust that he will bring us to his intended destination. Our eternal future rests in the hands of Christ.

Such was the case for Lazarus and his sisters in this passage from the gospel of John. Martha was reminded to trust Jesus in all things when the Lord raised her brother from the dead—not just "in the resurrection on the last day," but on the very day that Jesus came to Bethany.

While we can live in hope because of Christ, we also have the ability to die in hope. It is a blessed thing to live at peace because we know that our eternity is secure in Christ. It is a wonderful thing to share the joy of our salvation with other believers and to be able to encourage one another in the mutual hope we have in Christ.

Jesus says, "I am the resurrection and the life. Those who believe in me, even though they die, will live, and everyone who lives and believes in me will never die."

Saturday after the Fourth Sunday in Lent

Reflect on the scriptures studied this week with these questions in mind:

What theme(s) have I noticed in the scripture passages this week?

What do I anticipate learning in worship as the church gathers in community on Sunday?

How do I anticipate responding to God and his word in worship on Sunday?

What passage has God used to speak to me this week?

How is God calling me to a holier place in life during this Lenten season?

Lord, thank you for speaking through the scriptures in every generation. As our church gathers to worship on Sunday, draw us closer to yourself by uniting us around a common conviction by the power of the Holy Spirit. Amen.

The Fifth Sunday in Lent

Loving One:

Thank you for the Christian hope—that hope that gives your people the freedom to live life with assurance. Grant us grace to live at peace, knowing that you are the resurrection and the life and in you there is no death.

Deliver us, O God. Amen.

Monday after the Fifth Sunday in Lent

Reflect on the past week of personal worship and worship in community with these questions in mind:

What can I give up in order to spend time in closer communication with God?

How has the Lord spoken to me through the scriptures this week?

How is God challenging me to a fuller life in Christ during this Lenten season?

What insights did I gain through worship in community this week?

Thank you, O God, for a week of personal and corporate worship. Draw me closer to you as I reflect on those things you have revealed to me through the scriptures by the power of the Holy Spirit. Amen.

Tuesday after the Fifth Sunday in Lent

Read: Isaiah 50:4-9a

When I read this passage, I was reminded of a lady I know called "Granny." When Granny was young, her husband abused and abandoned her, leaving her to parent four children as a single mom in the 1960s. One of her sons suffered from AIDS and died a painful death in the early 1990s. Another son is mentally disabled and has required both inpatient and outpatient treatment over forty years of life. A third son left home early and only visits from time to time as his schedule permits. Granny's second husband (a man we all call "The Saint") now suffers with Alzheimer's disease. Granny also endured the brutal murder of a grandchild that she had raised as her own.

Through the years, Granny has experienced a few graces along the way and she clings to those events as gifts from God. She is thankful, even for her tragedies, and when asked how she's been able to deal with the many problems she's faced, she replies simply, "I am grateful to God for sustaining me. I just can't help but serve him." And she does just that. Granny is always the first to volunteer to lend a helping hand around the church, to pray with those who are discouraged, and to open her home to "anyone who needs a granny." She understands that, without her faith, she would have no hope—and her hope has been her one saving grace through it all.

The Servant described in this passage from Isaiah has known the pain of being cast aside. He has met with adversity and with God's help has stood strong in the face of insult and injury. His experiences have given him knowledge—for as he seeks "to sustain the weary with a word," he is able to relate intimately to their suffering through his own torment and affliction. The Servant is confident of one thing: he is never alone, for the Lord God is ever-present no matter the circumstance.

We all have two choices when we meet with the calamities of life: 1) we can choose the bitterness that leads to faithlessness or 2) we can choose the hopefulness that leads to service. This mystery of suffering reminds us that God is not just the friend who takes us by the hand and guides us when our eyesight is failing; but God is also the great, majestic Creator who reigns forever and reveals pieces of the big picture—snapshots of grace—along the way. That assurance gives me hope, even when there seem to be no answers in the midst of hardship and suffering. That hope should inspire us all "to sustain the weary with a word."

Wednesday after the Fifth Sunday in Lent

Meditate on Psalm 118:

O give thanks to the LORD, for he is good; his steadfast love endures forever!

Let Israel say, "His steadfast love endures forever."

Let the house of Aaron say, "His steadfast love endures forever."

Let those who fear the LORD say, "His steadfast love endures forever."

Out of my distress I called on the LORD; the LORD answered me and set me in a broad place.

With the LORD on my side I do not fear. What can mortals do to me?

The LORD is on my side to help me; I shall look in triumph on those who hate me.

It is better to take refuge in the LORD than to put confidence in mortals.

It is better to take refuge in the LORD than to put confidence in princes.

All nations surrounded me; in the name of the LORD I cut them off!

They surrounded me, surrounded me on every side; in the name of the LORD I cut them off!

They surrounded me like bees; they blazed like a fire of thorns; in the name of the LORD I cut them off!

I was pushed hard, so that I was falling, but the LORD helped me.

The LORD is my strength and my might; he has become my salvation.

There are glad songs of victory in the tents of the righteous: "The right hand of the LORD does valiantly;

the right hand of the LORD is exalted; the right hand of the LORD does valiantly."

I shall not die, but I shall live, and recount the deeds of the LORD.

The LORD has punished me severely, but he did not give me over to death.

Open to me the gates of righteousness, that I may enter through them and give thanks to the LORD.

This is the gate of the LORD; the righteous shall enter through it.

I thank you that you have answered me and have become my salvation.

The stone that the builders rejected has become the chief cornerstone.

This is the Lord's doing; it is marvelous in our eyes.

This is the day that the LORD has made; let us rejoice and be glad in it.

Save us, we beseech you, O LORD! O LORD, we beseech you, give us success!

Blessed is the one who comes in the name of the LORD. We bless you from the house of the LORD.

The LORD is God, and he has given us light. Bind the festal procession with branches, up to the horns of the altar.

You are my God, and I will give thanks to you; you are my God, I will extol you.

O give thanks to the LORD, for he is good, for his steadfast love endures forever.

Thursday after the Fifth Sunday in Lent

Read: Philippians 2:5-11

Recently, I revisited G. K. Chesterton's classic missive called *Orthodoxy*. The orthodoxy about which Chesterton writes isn't concerned with the Orthodox Church; rather, it is a Christian apologetic focused on right doctrine or "orthodox" teaching. Chesterton's book (and its forerunner, *Heretics*) have regained popularity among post-modern Christians because these books are as culturally relevant today as they were when first published one hundred years ago.

There are many in this generation who are concerned with orthodoxy. Although content with the ambiguous, the entire emerging church movement makes much of helping post-moderns seek the truth. I have friends in the Anglican Communion who are wrestling with what it means to be orthodox when seeking to balance the grace of God with the truth of the scriptures. Historically, in keeping with the teachings of Jesus, evangelicals have sought an orthodox understanding of faith as well.

Of all the groups focused on neo-orthodoxy, it seems that young evangelicals are particularly interested in the pursuit of truth and life anew.

One thing that's impressive about this group is that they have a firm grasp of the truth of orthodox faith encapsulated in this fact: there is no true orthodoxy *sans* orthopraxy. In other words, right teaching and belief must be accompanied by right practice or action for "faith by itself, if it has no works, is dead" (James 2:17).

This guidance on how to be Christian in the world because of one's belief in things not of this world is having a profound impact on servant ministry. Record numbers of young people are volunteering for mission service or are choosing professions that benefit the greater good. They consider it their responsibility to live out their faith each day in ways that make a difference for the Kingdom.

May we be inspired to a life concerned with both orthodoxy and orthopraxy and may God challenge his people as we learn to live faithful lives in accordance with the scriptures so that, "at the name of Jesus every knee should bend, in heaven and on earth and under the earth, and every tongue should confess that Jesus Christ is Lord, to the glory of God the Father."

Friday after the Fifth Sunday in Lent

Meditate on John 12:12-16:

The next day the great crowd that had come to the festival heard that Jesus was coming to Jerusalem. So they took branches of palm trees and went out to meet him, shouting, "Hosanna! Blessed is the one who comes in the name of the Lord— the King of Israel!" Jesus found a young donkey and sat on it; as it is written: "Do not be afraid, daughter of Zion. Look, your king is coming, sitting on a donkey's colt!" His disciples did not understand these things at first; but when Jesus was glorified, then they remembered that these things had been written of him and had been done to him.

Saturday after the Fifth Sunday in Lent

Reflect on the scriptures studied this week with these questions in mind:

What theme(s) have I noticed in the scripture passages this week?

What do I anticipate learning in worship as the church gathers in community on Sunday?

How do I anticipate responding to God and his word in worship on Sunday?

What passage has God used to speak to me this week?

How is God calling me to a holier place in life during this Lenten season?

Lord, thank you for speaking through the scriptures in every generation. As our church gathers to worship on Sunday, draw us closer to yourself by uniting us around a common conviction by the power of the Holy Spirit. Amen.

Palm Sunday

Exalted One:

You rode into Jerusalem on a donkey to much fanfare. The people heard that you were coming and cried out, "Hosanna! Blessed is the one who comes in the name of the Lord—the King of Israel!" How much they understood. How little they understood.

Deliver us, O God. Amen.

Monday in Holy Week

Read: John 12:1-11

When my wife and I visited Milan, Italy, we stood in line for tickets to an opera at *Scala*. We were proud to receive two seats at a fair price and we were excited to experience the art, architecture, and music at the famous venue. We got all dressed up and hailed a taxi to the performance.

About halfway through the first act, I noticed that the conductor that evening was directing this four-hour affair of the arts without referencing a score. As I settled back into my seat I thought to myself, "Well, I guess you don't need a map if you already know the way."

There was a lesson in this message for me—and perhaps for you. There is tremendous freedom in being well prepared. Preparedness allows us to make the most of every moment. Most importantly, being well prepared speaks to our faithfulness. This is especially true as we seek to be all that we can for the Kingdom of God each day.

On the day that we read about in this scripture passage, Mary's ministry to and witness for Christ showed that she had a wonderful grasp of who the Savior was. She had prepared for the day of his burial; however, in his presence, she felt drawn to worship at his feet and anoint him with the precious perfume she held in reserve. Jesus recognized her faithfulness and affirmed her act of love. Mary understood the importance of holding back nothing when it comes to serving the Christ.

Through our worship, our study, our prayers, and our communion with other believers we are grown into the witnesses that God has called each of us to be.

May God grant us grace to conduct ourselves in ways that are pleasing to the Father as we continue our journey through this Lenten season.

Tuesday in Holy Week

Read: John 12:20-36

Glorified Son of Man:

You told the crowd, "The light is with you for a little longer. Walk while you have the light, so that the darkness may not overtake you. If you walk in the darkness, you do not know where you are going. While you have the light, believe in the light, so that you may become children of light."

Give us grace, O Lord, to journey deliberately through this Holy Week, walking toward the light—even as we anticipate the darkness of your death on the cross.

Deliver us, O God. Amen.

Wednesday in Holy Week

Read: John 13:21-32

Betrayed One:

Give us grace to be true to you in all circumstances: acknowledging your holiness, celebrating your sacrifice, and proclaiming the truth of the gospel.

Deliver us, O God. Amen.

Thursday in Holy Week

Read: John 13:1-17

Humble Servant:

Teach us to follow your example. Show us that knowing what to do is important; however, doing what is good is essential.

Help us to know that servants are no greater than masters. Help us to master the art of service.

Help us to know that messengers are no greater than those who sent them. Help us to proclaim the message of eternal hope in you to every generation.

Deliver us, O God. Amen.

Good Friday

Read: John 18:1—19:37

Crucified Lord:

Give us pause. Help us to understand the significance of the sacrifice you made for us on this day. We bow our heads in reverence and fall on our knees at the foot of your cross.

Forgive us, O Lord. Amen.

Holy Saturday

Read: John 19:38-42

Entombed Lord:

On this day, we sit in silent meditation, reflecting on the week of agony and anticipating the day of Resurrection. Give us grace, Lord Jesus, to wait for your return. Amen.

Easter Sunday

Read: John 20:1-18

Christ is risen! Alleluia! Alleluia!

Epilogue

During the production of this volume, my friend and mentor, Dr. Robert E. Webber, passed away after battling pancreatic cancer. Bob was a leader in the worship renewal movement of the past twenty years and refocused attention on the early church as an appropriate model for ministry to post-moderns in the twenty-first century.

There were several things about Bob that demonstrated Christian character at its best. Bob was personable. With over forty books to his credit and a busy speaking, writing, and teaching schedule, Bob never missed an opportunity to sit with folks who were willing to share their stories. Through those conversations, Bob was able to shine a bright light for Christ and exert great influence for the Kingdom. By listening to the stories of others, Bob earned the right to share the greatest story ever told.

Bob was a man of honor and integrity who had a strong work ethic and always kept his commitments. A few weeks before he died, Bob wrote his colleagues and former students to say that he was still hard at work each day. As the Lord gave him strength, Bob recorded thoughts for upcoming projects. His goal was to fulfill all contractual obligations to his publishers before he passed away.

Bob was also an encourager and never wanted his students to be so overwhelmed that they might shut down under the pressure. He was a strong proponent of the message of Psalm 46, "Be still and know that I am God," and always erred on the side of grace. Bob sent me a note when I was busily writing my doctoral thesis, "It's a long obedience in the same direction," he wrote, "but sometimes we have to sit on a bench and catch our breath."

Bob will certainly be missed; however, he will continue to speak the message of the hope that each of us has in Christ Jesus. His insightful writings will bear strong influence on this generation and many to come. Those of us who knew Bob will remember fondly his call to the *Divine Embrace* that comes from renewing one's commitment to the Christian spiritual life.

Bob's legacy presents a challenge to me (and I hope to you!). May each of us strive to be the Christian witnesses that we are called to be so that our lives might shine as examples to this and to future generations. May our prayer each day be, *Lord Jesus Christ, you stretched out you arms of love on the hard wood of the cross that everyone might come within the reach of your saving embrace: So clothe us in your Spirit that we, reaching forth our hands in love, may bring those who do not know you to the knowledge and love of you; for the honor of your Name. Amen.*

About the Author

R. Kevin Johnson is Executive Director of Micah Ministries and has served in various denominational settings in pastoral, music, worship, and children's ministries. Dr. Johnson holds degrees in fine arts, music, worship, and spiritual formation and is a freelance author, consultant, and workshop leader in those fields of Christian leadership.